LAUNCHING YOUR BJJ COMPETITION JOURNEY AFTER 30

10 STEPS TO MAXIMIZE YOUR TOURNAMENT EXPERIENCE

GUSTAVO DANTAS

BJJ COMPETITION JOURNEY AFTER 30
10 STEPS TO MAXIMIZE YOUR TOURNAMENT EXPERIENCE

Published by
Perfect Bound
Marketing + Press

www.PerfectBoundMarketing.com

ISBN 978-1-939614-61-2

TABLE OF CONTENTS

INTRODUCTION

If you are reading ***Launching Your BJJ Competition Journey After 30*** then the chances are that you are an over 30 year-old Brazilian Jiu-Jitsu practitioner who is interested in getting involved in competitions. Competing for the first time can be a stressful experience if you don't know how to properly prepare yourself for this new challenge, especially when competition is not the main priority in your life. I wrote this book to help you in your new adventure and to share the shortcuts I have learned since I started my Jiu-Jitsu journey in 1989.

In the beginning of my career, I struggled to get positive results. I never competed as a white belt. I won one small tournament as a blue belt, and after a rough 0-5 beginning, I was able to become a World Champion in 1997 as a purple belt, a brown belt World Champion in 1998, and Black Belt Master World Champion at the age of 37 in 2012.

This book is not only my experience as a World-class competitor, but as a passionate teacher, father, entrepreneur, Certified Mental Coach, and Certified Life Coach. The content in this book will inspire you to accept even more challenges in your life for years to come, both on and off the mat.

The *10 Steps to Maximize Your Tournament Experience* that are shared in this book will bring you clarity to have a better understanding of how tournaments work and what you should do to prepare yourself more efficiently to increase the odds of achieving the outcome that you want, and enjoying your competition journey.

CHAPTER ONE

WHAT ARE THE BENEFITS OF COMPETING?

WHAT ARE THE BENEFITS OF COMPETING?

Besides the fact that competing will refine your Jiu-Jitsu game and keep you super focused on your training, I truly believe you can experience immense personal growth. When you step out of your comfort zone and challenge yourself by participating in tournaments, you learn a lot about yourself and how you handle your emotions when you find yourself in uncomfortable situations and under pressure. Competitions can bring out the best in people by developing and improving skills that are extremely useful in our personal and professional lives.

Competitions taught me to be even more disciplined. They motivated me to face my fears and anxieties and gave me the mental strength I needed in order to overcome adversities, failure, and all the "curve balls" that life throws at us when we least expect them. There are so many lessons to be learned from competitions, and I still learn more every time I compete; and you will too. This is why I believe that every Jiu-Jitsu practitioner should compete at least once for this priceless experience.

The reality is that we are all very busy with our personal and professional responsibilities, and I notice that a lot of the master's competitors, who are 30 years old and over, have either not been active for a long time or have never been involved in any competitive sports before which can lead to an overwhelming experience. I feel that a lot of us have that little itch to challenge ourselves, but too often the fear of failure assumptions and self-limiting beliefs hold us back from experimenting with new challenges in our lives.

We get bombarded with negative thoughts that can bring a lot of anxiety and convince us that competing is not a good idea. These thoughts include:

1. *"I am too old..."*

Being "too old" is no longer a plausible excuse. The number one organization in the world, the International Brazilian Jiu-Jitsu Federation, offers multiple divisions to competitors over 30 years old. You will NOT be competing against professional athletes. You will be testing yourself against other people who are of the same weight division and experience level as you.

Master 1 – 30 to 35 years old
(White, Blue, Purple, Brown, Black)

Master 2 – 36 to 40 years old
(White, Blue, Purple, Brown, Black)

Master 3 – 41 to 45 years old
(Blue, Purple, Brown, Black)

Master 4 – 46 to 50 years old
(Blue, Purple, Brown, Black)

Master 5 – 51 to 55 years old
(Blue, Purple, Brown, Black)

Master 6 – 56 to 60 years old
(Blue, Purple, Brown, Black)

There are a lot of other organizations promoting Jiu-Jitsu tournaments all over the world, but in this book, I will share with you tips and strategies that will help you to become more familiar with the events that run their competitions using the rules and regulations of the IBJJF, the highest authority of Jiu-Jitsu in the world.

2. ***"Am I good enough for this challenge? What if I lose? I don't want to disappoint my family, friends, coaches, and teammates!"***

You should never worry about whether you are going to win or lose, how others might perceive you if you don't meet their expectations, or if you don't meet the high expectations that you have for yourself. Before you allow any of these thoughts to cross your mind, just remember that losing will not make you any less of a person. As a parent, I believe that competition is a great way to lead by example, as it helps to teach kids about failure and success. It is important for them to realize that it's okay not to win, and in our everyday lives we have to accept that sometimes we will lose. We don't get every job we apply for or succeed at every endeavor. As long as you are committing to be the best that you can be with the tools and knowledge you have right now, regardless if it is in Jiu-Jitsu or your personal and professional life, then you are successful. When you are constantly getting out of your comfort zone, facing your fears and anxieties, and stretching your limits, I guarantee you will experience a great deal of personal growth as you go through your journey.

Do I have anything to lose by competing in tournaments?

In 2014, I started a project called, *How High Can You Fly?* I made a decision to go out of my comfort zone and accept a new challenge, which was to qualify to compete at the 2015 IBJJF Adult World Championship on May 30th and 31st in Long Beach, California. Starting in 2015, the adult black belt competitors needed a minimum amount of 50 points in the IBJJF ranking to be eligible to compete at this tournament, which means I needed to be active in the adult division.

There were a lot of factors that made this challenge extremely hard; not just the fact that I was 40 years old and eligible to compete in the masters 3 division, which means the injuries and their recovery from training are slower, but also my busy entrepreneur schedule consumed precious time.

Not surprising, a lot of people felt that I had a lot to lose in competing (especially in the adult division where the odds were against me). A tournament loss could compromise my status, as I am an established teacher in the United States with a lot of students. I also have a lot of worldwide support from the BJJ Mental Coach movement.

But do I have anything to lose by competing in tournaments?

Very often people will give me compliments about the competition challenges I have recently started to accept. Most of them say things like, *"You have guts, man!"*

Why do I have guts?

What makes me different than any other person who trains and competes in Jiu-Jitsu tournaments and accepts the big challenges? Is it because I am putting my status or my reputation on the line? No, it is my perspective! I ALWAYS remind myself, *"Gustavo, you have NOTHING to lose! This experience is a win-win situation!"*

In one year, I competed 11 times. I went to Abu Dhabi, Munich, Rome, Gothenburg, Zurich, Las Vegas, Long Beach, Irvine, and Torrance. I met great people and I was introduced to new cultures. I learned a lot about Jiu-Jitsu but the most important thing to me was that I learned a lot about myself! I learned how to deal with my emotions more efficiently as well as my failures, successes, wins, and losses.

Did I always think like that? I will be 100% honest… NO! As I like to say, *"We change opinions and beliefs all the time! Basic values like integrity, trust, honesty, fairness, and so forth don't change, but opinions and beliefs can be questioned and changed any time you want. This is a belief I personally changed."*

At one point in my life, my self-esteem was lower than it should have been. I cared and worried about what others had to say or think about me.

What is self-esteem?

"Self-esteem is our overall evaluation or appraisal of our own worth."

I had self-limiting beliefs that prevented me from doing certain things I wanted to do in different phases of my life. From a lack of training partners in my early days in Arizona to injuries, and from relationship issues to financial problems, my self-confidence was low. My fear of failure was holding me back not only in Jiu-Jitsu, but in my personal and professional lives as well. Here is the best analogy I can think of to best explain how I felt:

> *"I was driving forward with my emergency brakes on, but I didn't have the clarity to see it, release the brake, and drive*

at a normal speed. Sometimes I would get stuck and would not drive at all."

Have you ever felt like this? Having the feeling you are moving forward toward your goal but carrying a bunch of unnecessary weight? Or maybe not even moving forward at all? Do you feel like you are living your life way below your full potential? It's even worse when you are aware of it but you can't pull yourself together to perform to the best of your ability in life.

Here were some of the negative self-beliefs I had in the past that related to competitions and the truth behind it:

> *"Am I still good enough? Can I still win? I don't want to disappoint my family, friends, students, or fans."* (avoiding shame, embarrassment, criticism and judgment)

Can you relate to this thought?

Some people who have a very strong fear of failure are more motivated to avoid failing. Not because they can't handle the disappointment, anger, and frustration that comes with it, but because failing makes them feel ashamed or embarrassed. They feel people will criticize and judge them if they don't meet the their expectations.

Do YOU have fear of failure?

What about you? Let's take a look at some of the common patterns of fear of failure. I want you to think of the "big picture" though, not just Jiu-Jitsu, but in your personal and professional lives as well. Do any of these statements apply to you?

– You worry about what others think of you.

– You question if you are "good enough."

- You worry about disappointing others if you don't meet their expectations of you.
- In order to lower their expectations, you tend to tell people that you don't expect to succeed.
- You avoid doing something if you know you won't be able to do it well.
- You procrastinate on the things you really want to do because you don't believe you can do them.
- You avoid going out of your comfort zone.
- You get extremely frustrated when you don't meet your own high expectations.
- You sabotage yourself, find excuses, and blame life circumstances for preventing you from moving forward with a desire, goal, or a dream. (BE HONEST!)
- You are living your life way below your full potential and you are aware of it! You know you can do so much better.

OUCH! Okay, Take a deep breath now…

"Ok, Gustavo, it seems like I have some fear of failure. What should I do now?"

I am going to share with you three strategies to help you overcome your fear of failure:

1. **Accept that failure will happen.**

   Failure is not just acceptable, it's necessary for personal growth. Failure can make you or break you. It can motivate you to improve your skills and address the issue with a different approach. It can also help you to become mentally tougher and more resilient. It's all about how you interpret the "event".

"Life events should NOT define you as a person." YOU choose how you want to interpret a tournament loss, a relationship break-up, or a failed business attempt. You can respond to or react to the fact or the event. The choice is yours and only yours!

2. **Work on yourself.**

   One of my favorite public speakers, Jim Rohn, said, "Work harder on yourself than you do on your work."

   Invest in yourself! Work hard on your personal development in order to discover what is holding you back from being the best you can be. Find the true cause of your fear and resolve it!

   In my program *Inner Discovery for Outer Success* I share concepts, principles, and techniques that have helped so many people (including myself) to understand our fears and anxieties, and handle them in an efficient and positive manner.

   If you would like more information about my four-disc DVD, which is also available ON DEMAND, check it out online at www.thebjjmentalcoach.com.

3. **Embrace the fear of failure.**

   I have good news and bad news for you. The bad news is that negative patterns, assumptions, worrying, doubts, and insecurities associated with fear of failure do not disappear; they are a part of the human emotional experience that you can never get rid of.

The good news is that you can learn how to control it. I do have a fear of failure, but I don't let fear control my life and you shouldn't either!

How comes you are not scared of anything?

One day I was driving with my son, Jonathan (he was ten years old at the time), and out of nowhere he asked me, *"Dad, how comes you are not scared of anything?"* Surprised and confused I asked him, *"What do you mean?"*

Jonathan said, *"You always do whatever you want! You are never scared of anything!"*

I smiled and replied to him, *"That is where you are wrong, buddy. Daddy is scared of a lot of things, I just don't let fear control my life!"*

What about you? Do you let fear consistently control the decisions you make in your life? If so, what are you afraid of? What is the real reason you don't challenge yourself more consistently? Be honest with yourself. This might be a great opportunity to break the cycle and get out of your comfort zone.

In studying Mental Skills Training and Personal Development, you will increase your self-awareness, have more clarity to re-evaluate your self-limiting beliefs that are holding you back, and rationally (instead of emotionally) choose what action to take.

It is totally up to you. Now that you are aware of the fact you are driving with your emergency brake on, are you going to release it or keep it on? It's YOUR choice, my friend!

We are born with only two types of fear, fear of loud noises and fear of falling. All other fears were created by our own minds. Think about all the short- and long-term consequences of not facing your fears and anxieties; how much of your life journey are you missing out on? How many unused talents, skills, goals, and dreams are you going to take to the grave with you when you die? Life is too short and you only live once. Don't let fear control your life, "Feel the fear, and do it anyway!" Embrace your fear of failure.

CHAPTER TWO

I DON’T WANT TO BECOME A WORLD CHAMPION

I DON'T WANT TO BECOME A WORLD CHAMPION!

Often, people tell me, *"Yeah Gustavo, all this sounds good, but I'm not trying to become a successful World Champion or anything, I have a full-time job, wife, and kids."*

People have different perceptions of the meaning of success. You don't need to be a black belt adult World Champion in order to become successful. You could be a 40 year old white belt, competing for the first time in a local tournament. What do these two athletes have in common? Both are trying to be the best they can be within their limitations, commitment, time, and physical ability. You don't have to compete every month. In my school, I have plenty of competitors over 30 years old who compete only one to three times a year. As I mentioned earlier, I believe every Jiu-Jitsu practitioner should compete at least once.

Personally, I am a fan of the legendary basketball coach, John Wooden, and his approach to the meaning of success. It has made a huge impact on my life so I share his message any chance I can:

> *"Success is peace of mind, which is a direct result of self-satisfaction in knowing you made the effort to do your best to become the best that you are capable of becoming."*

If competing is something you would like to try out at least once, follow Nike's advice and *"Just do it!"* A very interesting book titled, *"The Top Five Regrets of the Dying"* written by Bronnie Ware, mentions that the most common regret of all, when people realize that their lives are almost over is:

1. *"I wish I'd had the courage to live a life true to myself, not the life others expected of me."*
2. *"I wish I hadn't worked so hard."*
3. *"I wish I'd had the courage to express my feelings."*
4. *"I wish I had stayed in touch with my friends."*
5. *"I wish that I had let myself be happier."*

What's your greatest regret so far and what will you set out to achieve or change before you die? What legacy would you like to leave on the planet when it is your time to go?

I want to leave a legacy that I lived an authentic life. I did whatever I felt was congruent to my values. I not only pursued my goals and dreams but I also inspired others to do the same, to face fears and anxieties, to fail, to be rejected, to fall down, but always to get back up for more action.

With that said, there are two days of the week when you shouldn't worry about anything, yesterday and tomorrow. So, live in the now! Life passes by too fast, enjoy it to its fullest. Let's get started!

RAY'S JOURNEY

I'm pushing 40 this year and I'm having the best time and looking forward to a competition. At 34, since my kids wanted to compete, I figured I should too. Since my first of many competitions I would say that competing has helped me stay focused with my diet and overall health. It also allows me to test myself to find out what I am able to put to use during a high stress situation outside of my own school.

Competition isn't for everyone but being able to continue in a sport into my 40s can also be rewarding beyond medals. My losses are a teaching moment for my kids (and myself) that it's OK to not come out on top. It keeps things in perspective for all of my family, as we all compete. Did I give 100%? Did I prepare my best? If I did that, then I can learn and come back and push forward just like in life.

– Ray Fuentes (40 years old)

CHAPTER THREE

WHY DO YOU WANT TO COMPETE?

WHY DO YOU WANT TO COMPETE?

A very important thing for you to figure out is why you want to compete. Some people may answer, *"Because I want to win the gold medal!"* No, no, no! Winning is an outcome, a result.

What is your purpose? Why do you want to compete? What is driving you to sacrifice time that you could otherwise be spending with your family and friends, but instead are training? Why are you investing your money on entrance fees, traveling expenses, seminars, DVDs, private classes, and so forth on this goal?

Some people enjoy the adrenaline of getting out of their comfort zone to challenge themselves. Some want to be an example to their children. Some want to test their skills and see how far they can go in Jiu-Jitsu. You need to dig deep and find your own reason.

Personally, I'm a competitive person, not necessarily just in Jiu-Jitsu though; I like to compete. I like to challenge myself and face my fears and anxieties. I love the feeling of self-satisfaction I get when I am done with a challenge, especially when I am at peace with myself knowing I did the best I could with the tools and knowledge I had in that moment. And above all, my main "WHY?" is my legacy.

WHAT WILL YOUR LEGACY BE?

Imagine you are at the funeral of a friend and your friend's family asks you to say a few words about their son on how you remember him and what his legacy was. Let's say you do and it goes well, and that night as you go to sleep you think, "What will be my legacy?"

That is what these next few pages are about, what will your legacy be? Maybe the story about my Worlds' experience can help you.

On May 30th, 2015 my, *How High Can YOU Fly* project became a reality. After competing in six tournaments and accumulating 51 points in the adult division point system, I had the privilege of competing in the 20th Edition of the IBJJF World Championship.

Going in to this tournament, I had been dealing with a serious injury in my left elbow. I took a cortisone shot before the Zurich International, my last tournament before the Worlds, but it didn't help much. The last two weeks of training leading to the Worlds were limited only to drilling, swimming, and running.

I won my first match against the Japanese competitor, Tatsuya Kaneko, by 6x0. My second match was against the 2015 Pan Champion, JT Torres, a competitor I've been a fan of for a long time. I was losing the match by 5x0, when during a scramble to get out of the side mount, I ended up dislocating my elbow. I suffered with terrible pain, but thankfully the medics were able to pop it back into place. I would love to tell you that I got back on the mat like the Warrior that I am, turned the match around and won. But that didn't happen at all. I was done! My 2015 Worlds journey ended there.

What would you have done in this situation? Would you have pulled out of the tournament? Would you have gone through with it? My "WHY" motivated me to keep me going with my challenge, my "LEGACY".

First, I want to make my son, Jonathan Dantas, and my family, proud of who I am and who I was as a human being when I die. Second, I want to be an inspiration for them and to everyone who appreciates my work. I want to inspire people to live life to its fullest, to live their dreams, to consistently challenge themselves by going out of their comfort zones, to grow as human beings, to feel the fear of failure, to embrace it, and do it anyway!

What will your legacy be?

I'm going to ask you to go to a "dark" place now. I would like you to picture your funeral. Are there a lot of people there? What are they talking about? Are they crying or rolling their eyes? Are they sharing meaningful stories about you?

Creepy, right? I'm just keeping it real with you because whether you like to hear it or not, one day you are going to die like everyone else.

How do you want to be remembered? What will you leave behind? Did you impact lives? What difference did you make in the world?

I'm going to share with you three key elements I have been using during the process of building my legacy and hopefully this will be useful to you.

1. *Values*

This is huge! Live in congruence with YOUR values! My number one value since I was a teenager has been FREEDOM OF CHOICE, which is why I chose to be an entrepreneur. I have freedom to choose whatever I want to do, whenever I feel like it. I had to work very hard (and I still do) to be able to live the life I dreamed of. I no longer need to ask permission for time off from my boss to go on a trip. I just do it!

My number two and three values are: INTEGRITY and TRUST. My mom taught me this very well. As soon as a person breaks those two values, they're done!

These are my top three values, what about yours? What do you value? Whatever your values are, live in congruence with them. If you want to live a truly authentic life, this is the first step.

Here is a list of values for reflection:

Achievement
Advancement and promotion
Adventure
Arts
Autonomy
Challenge
Change and variety
Community
Compassion
Competence
Competition
Cooperation
Creativity
Decisiveness
Democracy
Economic security
Environmental stewardship
Effectiveness
Efficiency
Ethical living
Excellence
Expertise
Fame
Fast living
Fast-paced work
Financial gain
Freedom
Friendships
Having a family
Health
Helping other people
Independence
Influencing others
Inner harmony
Integrity
Intellectual status
Leadership
Location
Love
Loyalty
Meaningful work

Money

Nature

Openness and honesty

Order (tranquility / stability)

Peace

Personal development/ learning

Pleasure

Power and authority

Privacy

Public service

Recognition

Relationships

Religion

Reputation

Security

Self-respect

Serenity

Sophistication

Spirituality

Stability

Status

Time away from work

Trust

Truth

Volunteering

Wealth

Wisdom

Work quality

Work under pressure

Other: ________

____

____

____

2. *Chase Your Passion, Not Your Pension*

I learned this phrase from the motivational speaker, Dennis Waitly. I know a lot of you are going to say, *"I wish it was that easy, I have to pay the bills!"*

Good point! Here is the truth though, it's NOT easy and it's NOT meant to be easy to live YOUR passion! I had to work full-time on my living and part-time on my dream, for years. Do you think I was making a living with Jiu-Jitsu and living my teenage dream straight away? You are wrong!

In 1999 I left Brazil. I moved to a different country with a different language, my tourist visa, two bags, and a couple thousand dollars just to pursue my dream.

I worked in construction, gardening, painting, house

cleaning, security and was even a driver… but I did it all with my dream of making a living with Jiu-Jitsu, in mind. This dream had been mine since I was 16 years old.

I don't tell you this to impress you, but to convey to you that you, too, can live your dream… as long as you understand that you must pay the price, you must take risks, you must face the fear of the unknown, and mainly take MASSIVE ACTION toward your goal!

What do you usually spend your days doing once you have come home from your full-time job? You have two options:

• Relax. Do you, watch some TV, play video games, and play on the internet for the rest of your free time

Or –

• Hustle! You work part-time on your dream! Whatever that is! Is it Jiu-Jitsu related? Then go train, lift weights, run, whatever. Is that the business you dream of? Well, go take classes, study, invest in yourself!

"Yes, Gustavo, that sounds good, but I need to spend time with my family."

Fair enough; hang out with the family, put the kids to sleep, and go work part-time on your dream. You might have to sacrifice a few hours of sleep to get where you would like to be. My question is, *"HOW BAD DO YOU WANT TO LIVE YOUR DREAM?"*

If you put in the time and effort, hopefully, one day you can have the "SHIFT", which means, your part-time job becomes your full-time job.

3. *Live your life purpose*

I believe everyone, including you, has a reason to be in this world. My life purpose is to inspire others to believe in their personal goals and dreams using Jiu-Jitsu as a channel to build greater self-confidence and self-worth while living a healthy lifestyle.

I only discovered my life purpose because I made a decision to invest in myself with personal development books, CDs, DVDs, attend seminars, and anything else that brought me clarity to see a bigger picture of this endless puzzle called life. A lot of the fundamentals, principles, and techniques I've learned from years of studying Mental Skills Training and Personal Development, plus my Jiu-Jitsu experience as a competitor and coach, I share in my program, *"Inner Discovery for Outer Success."*

Have you wondered about YOUR life purpose? Do you believe YOU have one? Do YOU believe YOU can make a difference in the world?

If you can utilize these three keys elements to build your legacy, you can live a fulfilling life that money cannot buy!

WHAT'S NEXT?

Now that you know WHY you are committed to this new challenge, you need to talk with your coach about your desire to compete. Some schools are more competition oriented than other schools that focus on self-defense, for example. This is not a matter of which approach is better or worse; it's about what school fits your needs.

Trust your coach's judgment!

If you already trust your coach by paying for membership in his school, you might as well trust him when he tells you that you are ready to compete. It's impossible for me to say how long you should wait until you compete because all schools have different approaches, teaching methodologies, and philosophies, not to mention the competitor consistency, athleticism, and other unique and individual factors.

The white belt division can be tricky, because there is a chance of a brand new white belt going against another brand new white belt or the brand new white belt can go against someone who is about to get his/her blue belt. It's just part of the game.

He said, *"YES!!!"*

At the moment that your coach says, *"Yes,"* for you to compete, it's time to take action. I am going to share with you the "10 Steps to Maximize Your Tournament Experience."

MICHAEL'S JOURNEY

"It was not easy for me to swallow my pride and the anxieties of being "the new/awkward guy" just barely starting out in a highly, athletically demanding martial art. But at my age, trying to keep up with my kids was starting to become quite the challenge, physically. Before I know it, less than a year in and I'm not only extremely passionate and cannot stop thinking about Jiu-Jitsu, but I'm competing successfully! Sure I regret not starting 15 years ago, but had I not started

at 32 years old I would've lived the rest of my years never knowing how fulfilling and accomplished this would feel… and I'm only just beginning."

– Michael Velasquez (33 years old)

CHAPTER FOUR

— STEP 1 —

CHOOSE YOUR WEIGHT CLASS

STEP 1: CHOOSE YOUR WEIGHT CLASS

You need to know what weight class you belong to. As I mentioned earlier, we are going to talk about rules and regulations of the International Brazilian Jiu-Jitsu Federation (IBJJF), during which you weigh in with your Gi (uniform) on, right before your first match.

I do not recommend doing any drastic weight cut because it can interfere with your performance immensely if you are not familiar with the process. Often, a competitor is already dealing with the nerves of the first tournament and adding the stress of making weight can really mess with a competitor's mind. It can even mess with the most experienced competitors' minds as well. Your mind should be focused 100% on your performance.

Choosing the proper weight class is extremely important. It doesn't matter if you are ready technically, conditionally, strategically, and mentally, because if you are not on weight, two things can happen:

1. Disqualification

IBJJF has a zero tolerance policy with regard to missing weight. If you don't make the weight in your first try, you don't even get to compete. Imagine that you get time off from work, pay for the registration, hotel, rental car, and food expenses, and then you don't get to compete! There is no one to blame but YOU. Take responsibility! I've never missed weight before and I'm not saying that I never will, because it can happen to anybody, but if one day this happens (I hope not) I will take full responsibility for not doing MY job.

2. *No gas in the tank*

I don't care that you drive a Ferrari; if you don't have gas in it, you will not drive anywhere! I personally start my nutrition program AT LEAST six weeks before I am going to compete in the featherweight division, which means I normally cut 15 pounds. I've been in situations that I've made weight but I did not perform to the best of my ability, because I had a bad weight cut, and I hear countless similar stories just like mine from students and friends.

Bottom line is, do your job and take responsibility for the weight class you choose and how you are going to make it and still have gas in your tank so you can perform to the best of your ability. By the way, weight cutting sucks! I am just giving you the heads up.

Take a look at the weight divisions of the IBJJF to see which one you belong in or you are at least the closest to:

WEIGHT DIVISIONS DIVISÕES DE PESO		JUVENILE MALE JUVENIL MASCULINO	ADULT, MASTERS MALE/MASCULINO	ADULT, MASTERS FEMALE/FEMININO	JUVENILE FEMALE JUVENIL FEMININO
ROOSTER GALO	MAX WEIGHT PESO MÁXIMO	118.0 lbs.	127.0 lbs	107.0 lbs	98.0 lbs
LIGHT FEATHER PLUMA	MAX WEIGHT PESO MÁXIMO	129.0 lbs	141.5 lbs	118.0 lbs	106.5 lbs
FEATHER PENA	MAX WEIGHT PESO MÁXIMO	141.5 lbs	154.5 lbs	129.0 lbs	116.0 lbs
LIGHT LEVE	MAX WEIGHT PESO MÁXIMO	152.5 lbs	168.0 lbs	141.5 lbs	125.0 lbs
MIDDLE MÉDIO	MAX WEIGHT PESO MÁXIMO	163.5 lbs	181.5 lbs	152.5 lbs	133.5 lbs

WEIGHT DIVISIONS DIVISÕES DE PESO		JUVENILE MALE JUVENIL MASCULINO	ADULT, MASTERS MALE/MASCULINO	ADULT, MASTERS FEMALE/FEMININO	JUVENILE FEMALE JUVENIL FEMININO
MEDIUM HEAVY MEDIO-PESADO	MAX WEIGHT PESO MÁXIMO	175.0 lbs.	195.0 lbs	163.5 lbs	143.5 lbs
HEAVY PESADO	MAX WEIGHT PESO MÁXIMO	186.0 lbs	208.0 lbs	175.0 lbs	152.0 lbs
SUPER HEAVY SUPER PESADO	MAX WEIGHT PESO MÁXIMO	197.5 lbs	222.0 lbs	No Max Weight Sem Peso Máximo	No Max Weight Sem Peso Máximo
ULTRA HEAVY PESADÍSSIMO	MAX WEIGHT PESO MÁXIMO	No Max Weight Sem Peso Máximo	No Max Weight Sem Peso Máximo		
OPEN CLASS	MAX WEIGHT PESO MÁXIMO	Check tournament rules Confira regras do campeonato	Free Livre	Free Livre	Check tournament rules Confira regras do campeonato

JOSEPH'S JOURNEY

"I will be turning 56 in a few weeks and I began training in Brazilian Jiu-Jitsu 11 ½ years ago at age 44. I started wrestling when I was 12 and wrestled competitively at the junior high, high school, college and post-college levels and I coached at the kids, high school and junior college level for 25 years. My last Wrestling competition was at age of 46, the same year I competed in my first Jiu Jitsu tournament. The transition from Wrestling to Jiu-Jitsu was very natural for me because I view them both as different yet similar forms of Grappling. I continue to grapple at my age because it's who I am and what I love to do, it's why I never need a vacation. The brief moments that I spend grappling each day bring me out of the past or future and place me in the Now and that is how I stay renewed, because it's impossible

to be thinking or worrying about something you did or must do when you are fighting for or fighting off a takedown or submission. My goal is to still be grappling when I'm 75. Grappling is my leisure activity, it's what I love to do because it brings me into the Now and that's something that I can't get from other leisure activities unless I start Grand Slalom Skiing. And that's not going to happen."

– Joseph Solorio (56 years old)

FIVE

– STEP 2 –

SIGN UP FOR THE TOURNAMENT

STEP 2: SIGN UP FOR THE TOURNAMENT

If finance is not an issue, sign up as soon as you can. Some people like to wait until the registration deadline just in case they get hurt, but the reality is that when training Jiu-Jitsu, there is always a potential for injury. Every time you sign up for the tournament, it makes the decision official. Now you are on the clock! You are officially committed to it! Tournaments with IBJJF rules and regulations have the registrations available online only, there are no registrations the day of the event.

A common question I get from my students is, *"I am only a few pounds over, what should I do? I don't want to be on the bottom of the division and end up going against guys who are a lot stronger."*

It's a valid point. Here is what I suggest:

- Sign up for a division that seems the most realistic to you, keep up with your training schedule, eat healthier, don't necessarily cut calories (I'm not a nutrition specialist to tell you what to do), and keep monitoring your weight. The IBJJF usually gives you a deadline to change divisions. If necessary, contact them to make the proper adjustment.
- If you are completely lost in what to do about your diet, either seek professional help, or if you can't afford it, research as much information as you can online.

PAUL'S JOURNEY

"I had no intention of competing when I started training Jiu Jitsu at the age of 37. I simply wanted to learn the art that had long intrigued me. As a lifelong athlete, however, it didn't take long for the competitive juices to start flowing. I soon wanted to test my new skills in a competitive arena. I wanted to prove to myself that I was still capable of performing under pressure. Sure, I wanted to win, but the outcome was almost secondary. I needed to know that I was still capable of placing myself in an uncomfortable scenario where victory and defeat were uncertain... With the first class instruction, both mental and physical, that I receive at Gustavo Dantas' academy, I am always confident in my preparation and abilities. All I have to do on the day of competition is show up and stay out of my own way. Looking to test yourself at an older age? There is no better medium than Jiu Jitsu."

– Paul Slaybaugh (40 years old)

CHAPTER SIX

— STEP 3 —

SET YOUR GOAL

STEP 3: SET YOUR GOAL

"If you fail to plan, you plan to fail."

Your goal should be to perform to the best of your abilitiy with the tools and knowledge you have. Sometimes your best you, will be enough to win, and sometimes it won't. But, in order to increase your odds of achieving the outcome that you want, you need to set your plan for the preparation of the tournament and establish more specific goals like your outcome goal, process goal and performance goal.

Outcome goal

Let's say you already know in which event you are going to compete, the date, a realistic time frame to prepare yourself for it, and so forth. Now you need to set yourself an outcome goal, which could be taking first or placing top four in your division, whatever you decide.

Now that you have established your outcome goal, it's time to set your process goal and your performance goal.

Process goal

The process goal is all about your preparation. It is during this process that you build your confidence. You focus on properly executing the techniques you want to implement in your game, in conjunction with your physical, strategic, and mental training.

The first question you need to answer to yourself is, *"Realistically, how many days of the week can I commit to training Jiu-Jitsu?"*

It's very tough for me to say how many times per week you should train, because we all have personal and professional responsibilities. Jiu-Jitsu is no different than anything else you would like to improve upon or excel at in your life; consistency is key. If I had to give you a number, I would say to train between three to four times per week. If you can train more, that is completely up to you. The best advice here is to listen to your body!

Any extra physical training you can get is great, as long as your body can handle it, but it is not meant to replace Jiu-Jitsu sessions, unless you are on a business trip and you have no option but running or lifting weights.

Do not underestimate your rest! Good sleep is crucial. Other activities that can help with your recovery are stretching, foam rollers, hot tubs, massages, and for people who see benefits to it, trips to a chiropractor can help.

INK IT, DON'T THINK IT!

Write everything down! In my DVD set, *"Inner Discovery for Outer Success,"* I talk about how much hard work the foundation of self-confidence is. When you KNOW that you did everything you could to be ready for your task, your confidence goes up!

But the truth is, setting the goal is not the main thing, but deciding how you will go about achieving the goal and committing to that plan is the main thing. You need to take full responsibility for your actions and the choices you make throughout the process of the goal setting. Otherwise, setting goals is just that… wishful thinking that will end in failure.

I am going to share with you a copy of one of my training schedules I used for my preparation to compete at the Abu Dhabi World Championship in April 2014. Every week I had to make adjustments to my schedule due to my professional duties. This is an example when I used a regular calendar. Every Sunday I would plan my week according to my schedule as realistically as I could. When I completed the task, I would mark down √, and if I didn't for some reason, I would use an X.

As an entrepreneur with other professional and personal priorities, many times things came up that took precedence. Injuries popped up along the way, and sometimes I needed to rest because I was just "beat up" from training. Sometimes I missed a training session. If this starts to happen consistently, you may want to review the goals you set as they may not be realistic to your current life style.

You will see that I had strength and conditioning sessions (S&C) plus swimming sessions when my schedule allowed me. Of course, the level of my competition is very different than the competitor in the white belt division.

The best advice I can give you is, don't set your expectations too high for your training routine like training twice a day every day, because when you don't meet your expectations, you can get overwhelmed with a feeling that you are not doing your job. Set your goal according to your reality!

See the following page for training schedules.

February 2014

Sunday	Monday	Tuesday	Wednesday	Thursday	Friday	Saturday
						1
2	3	4	5	6	7	8
9	10	11	12	13	14	15
16 TRAINING CAMP STARTS! →	17 AM-BJJ ✓ PM-SWIM ✓	18 AM-BJJ ✓ PM-S&C ✓	19 AM-BJJ ✓ PM-SWIM ✓	20 AM-BJJ ✗ PM-S&C ✓	21 AM-BJJ ✓	22 REST
23 REST	24 AM-BJJ ✓ PM-S&C ✓	25 AM-BJJ ✓ PM-SWIM ✓	26 AM-BJJ ✓ PM-SWIM ✓	27 AM-TRAVEL PM-BJJ ✓	28 PM-BJJ ✓	SEMINAR ILLINOIS

March 2014

Sunday	Monday	Tuesday	Wednesday	Thursday	Friday	Saturday
						1
2 REST	3 AM-BJJ ✓ PM-S&C ✓	4 AM-BJJ ✓ PM-SWIM ✓	5 AM-BJJ ✗ PM-S&C ✓	6 AM-BJJ ✓ PM-SWIM ✓	7 AM-BJJ ✓	8 REST
9 REST	10 AM-BJJ ✓ PM-S&C ✓	11 AM-BJJ ✓ PM-SWIM ✓	12 PAN	13 PAN NO TRAINING	14 PAN	15 NSA PUBLIC SPEAKING ACADEMY
16 AM-SWIM ✓	17 AM-BJJ ✓ PM-S&C ✓	18 AM-BJJ ✓ PM-SWIM ✓	19 AM-BJJ ✓ PM-S&C ✓	20 AM-BJJ ✓	21 PERSONAL DEVELOPMENT IN CALIFORNIA →	22
23 NO TRAINING	24 AM-BJJ ✓	25 AM-BJJ ✓ PM-S&C ✓	26 AM-BJJ ✓ PM-SWIM ✓	27 AM-BJJ ✓ PM-S&C ✓	28 AM-BJJ ✓ PM-SWIM ✗	29 REST
30 REST	31					

April 2014

Sunday	Monday	Tuesday	Wednesday	Thursday	Friday	Saturday
	AM-BJJ ✓ PM-S&C ✓	1 AM-BJJ ✓ PM-SWIM ✓	2 PM-S&C ✓	3 TRAVEL TO TAMPA PM-BJJ ✓	4 AM-BJJ ✓ PM-SPEAKING ✓	5 SEMINAR BJJ ✓
6 REST	7 AM-BJJ ✓	8 TRAVEL TO Abu Dhabi	9 REST	10 AM-BJJ ✓	11 UFC NO TRAINING	12 REST
13 AM-S&C ✓	14 AM-BJJ ✓	15 AM-BJJ ✓	16 AM-BJJ ✓	17 WEIGH IN	18 Abu Dhabi World Pro	19
20	21	22	23	24	25	26
27	28	29	30			

PERFORMANCE GOAL

Regarding the performance goal, it's time to put all your hard work into action. With performance goal, you focus on your personal standards. Let me share one personal example. In order for me to get over my mental block of passing the guard, I had to establish some performance goal. Here is one:

> *"Ok, I have been using these guard passes really well in training, I have been giving trouble to my training partners, I have been drilling a lot, but I haven't used in a tournament yet, I BELIEVE that now is the time to use it!"*

That was my first step to overcoming the fear of making a costly mistake during the competition, a big issue that was holding me back from performing to the best of my ability.

I wasn't focusing on my outcome goal, which for me, is ALWAYS going as far as I can go in the bracket. I was focusing on getting my Jiu-Jitsu better and being my best self on the mat more consistently.

As I started to accomplish my performance goals, I noticed that I started to gain greater self-satisfaction on my performances, which is one of the benefits of Mental Skills Training.

I noticed that every time I got out of my comfort zone, and tried a move that I didn't use often in tournaments because of my fear of making a costly mistake, I would get more self-satisfaction, regardless if the move worked or not, or regardless if I won or lost the match. I felt that I could be at peace with myself knowing that I TRIED! I didn't have to regret or dwell on the fact that I didn't go for it.

> *"Oh man, I should have tried that move, but I didn't because I was afraid to make a mistake that could lead to a loss!"*

Since I started doing that, I started to perform better, and I believe that I still have a lot of room to grow.

Here are a few other examples of performance goals.

> *"I want to pull guard quicker, because I have been pulling guard slowly on my past tournaments."*

> *"I want to manage my dominant positions better, positions such as the back. I want to make sure that if I take my opponent's back, either I submit him or at least he/she gets stuck in there. I have been messing up my back takes during my past few tournaments."*

> *"I have been playing my spider guard (for example) really well during training, but I haven't used in a tournament yet. My performance goal is to be able to use one of my attacks during my matches."*

There are so many different ways to set performance goals in Jiu-Jitsu, you just need to know what you want.

Let me share a quote from one of the most successful female tennis players ever in the World, Steffi Graf, winner of 22 grand slams, and 337 weeks on the top of the World ranking.

> *"You can't measure success if you've never failed. I was taught that if you really want to reach your goals, you can't spend any time worrying about whether you're going to win or lose. Focus only on getting better."*

She understood the importance of controlling the controllable, a topic that we are going to explore in the next chapter. She was focusing on her process and performance goals, not the outcome goals. Although we should set outcome goals, they are not the most important thing to focus on because you cannot control it.

SARAH'S JOURNEY

> *"Once you see yourself as a competitor, you will see yourself as an athlete and you will treat yourself as such. Every day, in some way, I focus on how to make myself a little better. Whether it's by learning Jiu-Jitsu techniques, increasing flexibility, gaining strength or taking care of my body with great sleep and nutrition, it is all to achieve my goal to*

compete at my best. By having a purpose to center and focus my Jiu-Jitsu, I also gave myself almost unending motivation to take care of my mind and body."

– Sarah Black (36 years old)

CHAPTER SEVEN

— STEP 4 —

DON'T FOCUS ON THE OUTCOME

STEP 4: DON'T FOCUS ON THE OUTCOME

This is HUGE!!! Don't worry if you are going to win or lose! This is very important during the process of preparation for the tournament. You need to focus on things YOU can control. As a matter of fact, this is tip number two of my program, *"Inner Discovery for Outer Success: Control the Controllables."*

You must focus on things that you can control such as your nutrition, your rest, your conditioning, techniques you want to improve, your mental preparation, and your performance.

Anytime you put focus on things that you can't control such as the outcome of the tournament, it will lead to muscle tension, anxiety, and most likely not performing to the best of your ability.

I'm not saying that you can't win with muscle tension and anxiety, but it will be extremely challenging to reach your full potential and to be your best-self on the mat.

EXERCISE

Make a list of things that you can control and a list of what you can't control.

Here are examples of things you CAN control:

- Techniques you want to learn, develop, and implement in your game
- Conditioning
- Strategy

- Mental Preparation
- Nutrition
- Rest

Here are examples of things you CANNOT control:

- Level of your competition
- Assumptions of what people might think if you don't win
- Fear of disappointing coaches, teammates, friends, and family
- Past undesired outcomes and poor performances
- Unqualified referees
- Delayed tournament schedules

Now take time to create your own list of things that you CAN control. This is the list that you should focus on.

____

____

____

____

____

____

____

____

____

____

Now take time to create your own list of things you CANNOT control and put these out of your mind.

____

____

____

____

____

____

____

____

____

____

PERSEVERANCE

I understand that you are probably not trying to be a World Champion, but this statement from the greatest Jiu-Jitsu competitor ever, the ten times World Champion Roger Gracie, should be applied to any endeavor of your life.

> *"My greatest quality is perseverance. You need to insist and believe in what you want until the end. My defeats pushed me to keep trying to be the best."*
>
> – Roger Gracie

INK IT, DON'T THINK IT

Remember, setting goals is not the main thing, but deciding how you will go about achieving them and committing to the plan is. You need to take full responsibilities for your actions and choices that you will make throughout the process of the goal setting.

If you set up your plan, take action on it, not for just a week or two, but until your goal is reached! Perseverance is a huge part of your journey.

When you have a conviction that you did everything you could to be ready for your task, and you are sure you are 100% prepared, you become more confident, and you will have a better chance of performing to the best of your ability and reaching your full potential. Hard work DOES pay off!

Winston Churchill said, *"Continuous effort — not strength or intelligence — is the key to unlocking our potential."*

BOBBY'S JOURNEY

"Adopting the BJJ lifestyle and competing in tournaments at the age of 30, has been a transformative process for me — way beyond the mats. I could tell you all about how exciting it is to learn a new move but what's most interesting is my progression off the mat. In order to be well-prepared for a tournament I need to train a lot, eat well, sleep so I can recover and maintain my professional work life in a way that does not interfere with my BJJ goals and just general life. What I've discovered since beginning my journey in BJJ, 18 months ago, is that I lost 20 pounds without trying. The commitment to training naturally allowed me to take great care of my health and sharpen my mental state. This has also allowed me to progress in my profession because I've needed to adhere to a stricter schedule with zero time to

waste. The desire of needing to perform well on the mat has improved my thought process to where I feel relaxed and composed every single day after training. I can confidentially say competing has helped me approach life's challenges and opportunities without fear of failure."

– Bobby Green (32 years old)

CHAPTER EIGHT

— STEP 5 —

LEARN THE RULES AND REGULATIONS

STEP 5: LEARN THE RULES AND REGULATIONS

This is very important! You don't want to train hard for the tournament and end up being disqualified for an illegal move or a series of penalties that can lead to your disqualification, i.e. illegal grips, stalling calls, and so forth. Or even worse, you don't even get to compete because your Gi is too short, the patches are placed in the wrong spot or they are a different color. A complete set of rules can be downloaded at www.ibjjf.org. The International Brazilian Jiu-Jitsu Federation also offers a rules clinic before some events, if you would like to get more educated on the rules. Here is some basic information including the point system and the duration of the match that you should know:

POINT SYSTEM

Takedowns: 2 points

Knee on the belly: 2 points

Sweeps: 2 points

Passing the guard: 3 points

Mount, Back Mount or Back Take: 4 points

DURATION OF THE MATCH

Master 1 (30-35 years old)

White Belt: 5 minutes

Blue Belt: 5 minutes

Purple Belt: 6 minutes

Brown Belt: 6 minutes

Black Belt: 6 minutes

Master 2 and above (36 years old and over)

All Belts: 5 minutes

NOT KNOWING THE RULES

A few years back during the IBJJF Long Beach International Open, I was watching the end of a blue belt match since one of my students was on deck to compete.

Imagine it is the final minute of your match, and you are inside someone's open guard. You are winning by 2x0, what would you do? Would you try to pass the guard? Or would you stall the match until the end?

This competitor chose stalling, which is not the problem. Stalling is part of the game and you must know the rules so you know how to use it in your favor. The problem is that he didn't know what the referee had said. The referee said, "Lute!" which means fight! But he thought that the referee told him to stop, which is "Parou!" He stopped moving, and his opponent swept him, tied the score, and won the match because of the stalling call.

CHARLES' JOURNEY

Why do I like to challenge myself with training?

"My motivation for training is I like to constantly challenge my mind body and soul. For me Jiu-Jitsu is a parallel world to the corporate world I face every day. I also enjoy sharing my Jiu-Jitsu learning experience with my family. I think I am very fortunate enough to also have the same hobby with my wife and children. It brings great pleasure to be able to share the competition stage with them, in success or failure."

Why do I enjoy Competing?

"One not only faces challenges and fears during competi-

tion but I face those same challenges and fears with my career. I feel competition makes me more prepared when dealing with those same competitive challenges at work, such the anxiety and fear of failure. I am more comfortable now when I have present before a large audience because I have learned the required coping skills and am better prepared, to deal with those negative feelings."

How important to you is competition*?*

"For me competition is of utmost importance because I need a place to measure my progress in Jiu-Jitsu. It is not a place for the ego but it is the testing ground for your craft. I Every time before I compete I ask myself "My WHY determines my WHAT and my WHAT determines my HOW. What is your WHY to succeed Charles?" This is a question that one has to find the answer to themselves, and if you can find the answer you will know why you seek out competition."

– Charles Bann (40 years old)

CHAPTER NINE

— STEP 6 —

PREPARE YOURSELF MENTALLY

STEP 6: PREPARE YOURSELF MENTALLY

You might be surprised by how your adrenaline is going to kick in on the day of the tournament, so do not underestimate it. Trust me on that! You need to prepare yourself mentally for the time before the tournament and after the match.

Athletes have the feeling they need more cardio or drill more, buy more instructional DVDs, and invest in private classes. These can absolutely help, but all good physical, technical, and strategic training must be accompanied by good mental training. Mental skills, just like physical skills, need to be practiced.

There are many specific mental skills that contribute to success in Jiu-Jitsu and other areas of our lives including, psychological skills techniques that help us make adjustments to our actions, thoughts, feelings, and physical sensations and improve our performance on the mat. MST (Mental Skills Training) refers to the systematic and consistent practice of mental skills with the purpose of three things: Enhancing performance, gaining greater self-satisfaction, and increasing enjoyment.

WHAT IS "INNER DISCOVERY FOR OUTER SUCCESS?"

"Inner Discovery for Outer Success" is not a program that promises gold medals. As a matter of fact, it is not about winning or losing. This program is designed to help competitors discover what negative patterns are holding them back from performing to the best of their abilities and achieving the success they desire.

The reason it is not about winning or losing, it is because you can have a very good performance and still lose the match because you made one tiny mistake. Sometimes you can even have a poor performance and win. This is one of the reasons why you should not focus on the outcome of the tournament, as it is something you cannot control. You need to focus on your preparation and your performance. If you do that, you will have better odds to achieve the outcome you want.

The reason why I am so passionate about overcoming mental blocks in competitions is simple. I've been there before, and it sucks! I've been prepared technically and physically, but not 100% mentally. As a result, I had a hard time performing to the best of my ability.

So many times I felt frustrated after a match because I knew I could have done so much better than I showed. I kept telling myself, *"That was not me there, I didn't perform the way I practiced."* If you can't relate to this because you haven't yet competed, think about any situation you went into with full intentions of doing your best. It could be a big test or a job interview, but for some reason, your nerves got the best of you and you could not deliver. Something was holding you back. Whether in Jiu-Jitsu, your personal life or your professional life, you need to discover what it is and deal with it.

RESPOND OR REACT

In *"Inner Discovery for Outer Success"* I focus on fundamentals, principles, and techniques, including five tips that will help you discover what is holding you back from performing to the best of your ability, reaching your full potential, and achieving the success that you desire. One of my favorite topics is the "respond or react" principle, which you will use not only after the tournament, but anytime you believe this concept can be applied to other areas of your life.

In life there are only two ways to deal with a fact or an event. Even though these two words sound similar, reacting to a fact and responding to a fact are two different actions.

1. ***React: When you use your emotions and often react irrationally.***

   Have you reacted or even over-reacted to an episode in your life? Have you ever felt so frustrated that you kept dwelling on the fact over and over in your head, to the point that you couldn't even sleep?

2. ***Respond: When you use your intellect to respond rationally.***

   In learning how to respond, instead of react, you are a taking a big first step towards becoming more emotionally mature, a term that is not often used. Emotionally mature people deal with reality in an up-front, ethical, positive, and rational manner.

You must keep this very important concept in your mind. The fact cannot be changed, only your response to the fact can be changed. Mental Skills Training is for life!

If you would like more information about the program, please visit www.thebjjmentalcoach.com

HEATH'S JOURNEY

"As an older athlete the reasons that I compete are somewhat different now than earlier in my competitive career. I now compete to try and find my personal physical, mental, and technical limits. Competing on the biggest stages puts me in direct contact with fears and anxieties that many people try and avoid. I get satisfaction in getting comfortable with these uncomfortable situations. I feel more alive on competitions days. I also find that putting a competition on the calendar creates structure and focus too many other areas of my life. During a training camp I tend to eat better, sleep better, have more focus, and general live a healthier lifestyle than when I am not competing. My competition goals are as much about preparation for a tournament as they are competition day itself. I always try to embrace the grind of a training camp and find my limits in the process. Competitions now are a way for me to measure my preparation and performance against my best self."

– Heath Flicker (42 years old)

CHAPTER TEN

— STEP 7 —

SET YOUR GAME PLAN

STEP 7: SET YOUR GAME PLAN

A very important key part of increasing the odds of achieving the outcome you want in a tournament is developing your game plan. This topic can be a challenging one for me to share with you because schools have different approaches, teaching methodologies, and philosophies. You should consult your coach to help you come up with a competition game plan, but I would like to share with you the successful approach I use with my students.

One of the approaches is an analogy that I make about the similarity between Jiu-Jitsu and football. If you find this analogy valuable, it can help you figure out your game.

PLAY JIU-JITSU LIKE A QUARTERBACK

I have this concept called, *"Play Jiu-Jitsu like a Quarterback."* It takes a long time to become a great quarterback, it takes a long time to master a playbook. Inside a playbook aree different formations such as, shotgun, I-formation, split back, and so forth. Each formation leads to different plays based on how the defense is positioning itself.

The quarterback must be analytical about his formations. He needs to understand all the fundamental key points of the system he is playing and break them down to a science, mastering not only his formations, but common patterns that his opponents' defense uses when attempting to stop his plays. He needs to understand where his players must be positioned on the line of scrimmage before the play starts in order to have better odds of a successful play. When he sees that everyone is in the right position, he can now start the play.

If for some reason, one of his players is not positioned properly, like a lineman hanging out and not paying attention, there is a good chance of the play being compromised and decreasing the odds of succeeding in the chosen play.

If you want to be a good or even great Jiu-Jitsu player, you need to build a solid playbook and master it as well. This, too, takes a long time. Inside your playbook you will have different formations such as, Mount, Half-Guard, Spider-Guard, and so forth. Each formation will lead to different plays, based on how the defense is positioning itself.

Try to imagine your brain being the quarterback, and the parts of your body being the players; hands, feet, head, hips, etc. You need to understand all the fundamental key points of the system that you are playing and break them down to a science, mastering not only your formations, but common patterns that your opponents are going to use in an attempt to stop your plays. You need to understand where your players must be positioned before the play starts in order to increase the odds of having a successful play. When you see that your players are in the right position, that all the grips are correct, and your legs and hips are exactly where you want, you can then start the play.

If for some reason, one of your players is not positioned properly, such as a wrong grip or no grip in a De La Riva guard, there is a good chance of the play being compromised and decreasing the odds of succeeding in the play. If you are not ready to defend yourself, you are not ready to attack.

DO YOU HAVE A GAME OR DO YOU KNOW MOVES?

There is a big difference there. It's very common for beginners to know different moves, but not how to put them together. My suggestion for your game plan is to pick a system that you feel the most comfortable. It is most likely going to be the one that includes your high percentage moves. Let's talk about guards for example. Answer the following questions:

Which of your guards gives the most amount of trouble to your training partners?

What are your high percentage attacks?

Let's say your answer is Spider Guard for example. How can you improve your knowledge of this specific formation? Here are three steps:

1. Understand all the necessary key points to maintain the guard. For example, how you are going to position your body, your legs, and your grips.
2. Work on your awareness! Every time your opponent gets rid of one of your key points, stop what you are doing and get it back as soon as possible. Start to recognize common patterns that people use when they are trying to pass your Spider Guard. When you improve your awareness, you can anticipate yourself and minimize the chances of your opponent succeeding at his attempt.
3. Choose your plays wisely! The defense will use a lot of different approaches when passing the Spider Guard, including:

   – Standing, leading with the right leg

- Standing, leading with the left leg
- Kneeling with the right knee up
- Kneeling with the left knee up
- Both knees down
- Different grips

As you can see, you can be very analytical about your game, and it takes a long time to build and master your playbook. You can use this approach when you're learning a new system, like the Side Mount.

What are the key points to maintain the Side Mount?

You will have different variations that can be used, attacks based on how the defense is positioning itself, and so forth.

Now, what about when you are on the bottom?

What is the best way to handle and hopefully escape the Side Mount?

Use the awareness that you developed when playing top to the bottom and vice-versa.

What if your opponent opened up and you took the mount?

Now you are playing the mount system and so on.

It all comes down to how well you can put all the systems that you know, together. Jiu-Jitsu is no different from anything in life that you want to be good at. It takes time, consistency, and persistence. With good coaching, you can definitely speed up your process of building a solid playbook.

Talk with your coach about the type of formation or system you should focus on for your next tournament. As you start getting more experienced and you accumulate more knowledge, you will have more systems to audible to, if your opponent shuts your A plan down.

I hope this approach brought clarity to enable you to figure out your game, and to come up with a game plan for your upcoming tournament.

NIGEL'S JOURNEY

"Like many others, I decided to train Jiu-Jitsu for the physical workout, the need to learn something new, the camaraderie etc. In this sport you get these continuously and it is highly satisfying and fulfilling. The big question for me was whether to compete. What benefits would I get from competing versus just training? Is it worth facing the anxieties, fears and inhibitions I have?

It took me a while to answer these, but here are my reasons: It gives me a great platform on which to analyze and improve my technique. The challenge of competing lifts my level of performance and improvement. The goal setting installs a sense of accomplishment, but above all it gives you a sense that you deserve and did everything you can to win, which is much more satisfying than wining in itself."

– Nigel Kurtz (37 years old)

CHAPTER ELEVEN

— STEP 8 —

KEEP IT SIMPLE

STEP 8: KEEP IT SIMPLE

Here are a few important reminders important for the day of the event and even the day before the competition. First, this is not the best time to try out a different food or drink because you have heard that it will give you more energy. Don't try anything new, because you never know how your body is going to react to it. Keep it simple!

Don't change your warm up or training routines. Don't do things you are not used to. Once I saw one of my students at the tournament and he told me, *"Gustavo, my legs are so sore!"* I asked him why, and he said, *"I ran for 45 minutes last night to get in better shape!"* Running was not part of his normal preparation, his body was not used to it and responded .

Ok, running, lifting, or training hard the night before the tournaments will not help you get in better shape. If you are doing any light to moderate intensity activity, it should be because you have to watch your weight or you just want to break a sweat. The last few days before the tournament should be for maintenance only. Personally, if I don't have to, I won't do anything the day before, but it's optional.

TOURNAMENT SIMULATION

Here is the tournament simulation process I do the day before a competition. I only use this process when I am cutting weight to compete in the featherweight. If I am competing in the lightweight division, I still like to do it, but I don't have to be very strict with my simulation.

In order to do this process efficiently, it needs to be adjusted according to what time you will be competing. If you are going to compete in the morning, the process I am going to describe will be enough, but if you are going to compete at 5 p.m. for example, you might have to add more meals to the equation. Here is the process:

- Wake up at the same time you are going to wake up on the day of the competition and to go to bed the same time as well, if possible.
- Check your weight before breakfast (the same breakfast you are going to have on competition day).
- Check your weight after breakfast.
- See how much time it takes you to digest your breakfast. Most likely, within a two-hour window, you will have to go to the bathroom again, then check your weight once more. The more you do this process, the more you get to know how your body works.

Some people may say, *"Dude that is too much work!"* Well, you cannot control the outcome of the tournament, but you can influence the result by doing the little things that a lot of people are not willing to do. When you do these little things, you increase the odds of achieving the outcome that you want, though nothing is guaranteed.

ARRIVE EARLY

This one should be a no brainer, but it's not, and some of my students drive me crazy with this! If you are supposed to compete at 10 a.m., don't show up at 10 a.m.! Make sure that you arrive at least one hour before. I personally like to arrive two hours before. There are times when things happen that are out of your control, from a flat tire or bad traffic, to your division actually starting ahead of schedule, which can happen often at the IBJJF events. If you don't plan to get there early, you may end of getting there late!

Make sure you have time to check your weight before your official weigh-in. If for some reason you are overweight, at least you have spare time to do something about it. The tournament offers a test scale in the warm-up area. Be aware of one very important thing, when you step on the official scale. You have one chance to make weight! If you don't make weight on your first attempt, you will be disqualified. Even though you might have checked your weight on YOUR scale, that is not the official one, and very often they don't match, so be careful.

In one incident, a black-belt friend of mine who hadn't competed in years stepped on the scale wearing his shoes and went over the weight limit. Not knowing about the updated rules he said, *"Oh, let me remove my shoes."* The mat coordinator replied, *"I'm sorry sir, you are done, you only have one chance!"* and he was disqualified.

At the Long Beach International Open, October 20, 2014, I was scheduled to compete at 11 a.m. I was finishing my warm up when they called me to compete at 10:20 a.m. I like to warm up in one Gi and compete with another one, especially if I'm very close to my weight limit, because the Gi can get a little wet and add weight to it. I had to scramble to switch Gis, and run to check-in to compete. Luckily for me, everything worked out fine, simply because I arrived early.

WARM UP

Another reason you should arrive early is to have time for a proper warm up. As far as I know, I have never seen a school where you step on the mat for the class, shake hands, and go from 0-100 miles per hour in a sparring session. Many injuries can happen regardless in Jiu-Jitsu; imagine if you are not properly warmed up. Whatever you do, just remember to keep it simple.

The warm up is not just a time to prepare yourself physically for the competition, but a very import time to prepare yourself mentally, to get into your zone and focus on your performance.

EVENT CHECK LIST

Here is an alphabetical list of what I personally take to a tournament:

- Extra underwear (if you have to run to cut weight, wet underwear can add weight)
- Headphones (if you like to listen to music)
- I.D. (mandatory to compete)
- Mental Training log (include all my notes and positive affirmations)
- Sauna suit (for emergency weight cut)
- Snacks
- Scale (if you are travelling)
- Two Gis (Gis can rip during competition)
- Towel (if you have to cut weight)
- Water

Why is my list so long? I've seen and I've been through a lot in my Jiu-Jitsu competition journey and witnessed the disappointments when these items were not with a competitor at a tournament.

JODY'S JOURNEY

"Competition does not come naturally for me, especially at 35. Like most people my age, I have a myriad of excuses to bow out of a tournament. My wife, kids, jobs, this holiday, that vacation, a big project at work, a bigger project at home; the list can go on and on, yet something always draws me back to the brackets… Competing makes me feel alive. There is a unique feeling of excitement and fear that comes from competition that I did not realize was missing once I got older. I was so caught up in being a husband, father and worker bee that the primal competitive nature of my being was left dormant. This rejuvenated sense of self has cascaded throughout all aspects of my life, reducing timidity, increasing confidence and letting me know that 30 was not a ceiling, nor will 40 or 50 be. I credit Jiu-Jitsu and competition for my resurgence, from pulling me off the path of a cookie cutter life and to remembering who I was and understanding who I could be."

– Jody Smith (35 years old)

CHAPTER TWELVE

— STEP 9 —

CONTROL THE CONTROLLABLES

STEP 9: CONTROL THE CONTROLLABLES

The waiting area is called the Bull Pen and is where the competitors wait to be called to compete. The waiting game can be nerve wracking as you can often be bombed with negative thoughts such as, *"Did I train hard enough? Man this guy won a bunch of tournaments. Can I beat him? I have to win, I don't want to disappoint my family, friends, teammates and coach..."*

WAIT! WAIT! WAIT! Control the controllables, focus on things you can control. By this point, the only thing you can control is your performance!

Do you remember when I mentioned that hard work is the foundation of self-confidence? When you have the conviction that you did everything you could to be ready for your task, you followed your plan, and you went to most of the classes that you committed yourself to, there will be no doubt you did the best you could to be ready for the tournament.

Remind yourself, *"My goal is to perform to the best of my ability with the tools and knowledge I have right now. If I can do that, I have better odds of achieving the outcome I want."* Again, sometimes your best is enough to win, sometimes it is not, but I can guarantee you one thing, if you keep your mind open, you will learn a lot from this experience.

Every time irrational thoughts like doubts, insecurities, and assumptions attack you, take the following steps:

1. Stop and take a deep breath.

2. Question the thought, *"Is this thought rational or irrational? Do I have control of it or not?"*
3. Respond to the thought in the most positive and rational way possible. If it is a thought you can't control such as, *"What if I don't win?"* snap out of it and keep focusing on your performance!

SELF-REGULATION

The ultimate goal of Mental Skills Training is self-regulation—the ability to work toward goals by effectively monitoring and managing your own thoughts, feelings, and behaviors.

Self-Regulation and Mental Skills Training are not just for a Jiu-Jitsu tournament, they are for everyday life! Every day each one of us is fighting some type of internal battle that no one else knows about. It could be related to your personal or professional life. Every human being has his own dark passenger. This dark side includes, negative thoughts, insecurities, doubts, and assumptions. The average human being has an average of 50,000 thoughts per day, and 70 to 80% of them are negative! We don't realize how much we judge and criticize not only others, but also ourselves!

We all have a dark passenger who talks crap to us and makes us think, *"Am I good enough? Do I deserve this? Am I capable of accomplishing what I want?"*

I have good news and bad news for you. The bad news is that your dark passenger, the voice that constantly talks crap to you with doubts, insecurities, and assumptions, will never go away. But the good news is that you can learn how to control that voice and re-direct your thoughts. This is exactly how my program, *"Inner Discovery for Outer Success"* helps competitors who are dealing with the mental blocks that prevent them from being their best selves on the mat.

BRIAN'S JOURNEY

"Who says you can't teach an old dog new tricks? I started training with Gustavo at the age of 33 and started competing one year later.

I never gave age much thought until after a couple injuries and being promoted to blue belt. Until then I never considered age as a factor in competing. Now I just have to be more strategic about how I train for competition and when I am going to compete. It is important for me to do so.

I have always been competitive in whatever I chose to do, and for me age is not a factor that will prevent me from being competitive. Competing gives me a chance to test the skills.

I train every day. It gives me a goal to focus on and keeps training interesting by bringing new goals. I hope you will find the motivation to compete and the enjoyment well after 30 like I have after training with, and competing under, Gustavo Dantas as a white, blue, and soon to compete as a purple belt as well.

I can say his guidance, not just as a coach but as a certified mental coach, has directly contributed to my success on and off the mat. I am sure you will find success of your own if you follow through with the steps outlined in this book."

– Brian Wade (39 years old)

CHAPTER THIRTEEN

— STEP 10 —

SHOW TIME!

STEP 10: SHOW TIME!

Now it is time to display all of the hard work that you put in from the school mat to the competition mat. The Staff, also called the mat coordinator, will call you, check your Gi, check your weight, and if everything is ok, he will take you to the mat.

After your first tournament, it will be easier to visualize the whole process, from walking into the gymnasium, to the waiting, to the beginning of the match and having your arm raised. Does it happen all the time that you win? No, but why would you put an image of an undesired outcome in your head.

Locate your coach before the match. Usually tournaments are loud, with a lot of people screaming, and having multiple teammates trying to be the coach can be distracting. Do the best you can to listen to the main voice that is there to coach you.

If you have multiple matches, stay hydrated and do the best you can to focus on the now. For example, if you have four matches and you just finished your first one, don't focus on your third or fourth possible match because you don't even know if you are going to get there. One match at a time!

If you are able to perform to the best of your ability with the tools and knowledge you have at the moment, you will be proud of yourself regardless of the outcome of the tournament. Remember one thing in Jiu-Jitsu, you can't lose, you can only learn and grow. It's a win-win situation.

LOLEINI'S JOURNEY

"Jiu-Jitsu has changed my life. Since 2013, I have trained and competed in many Jiu-Jitsu competition. It has taught me to eat healthier in order to do well in competition. I have lost over 40 lbs to get down to my goal weight. Competing has helped me to build my confidence. Also, I want to set an example for my daughter and other women that they can do anything even at the age of 37. It's not too late to join Jiu-Jitsu."

– Loleini Emmsley (37 years old)

CONCLUSION

The best advice I can give you from the bottom of my heart is to ENJOY THE JOURNEY! This is not just in Jiu-Jitsu, but also in your personal and professional lives.

If you have a goal or a dream, go after it! If one of your goals in Jiu-Jitsu is competing, not necessarily becoming a World Champion, again, just do it. We are all super busy with our personal and professional responsibilities, and if you are only able to compete once or twice a year, so be it, but don't let fear of failure and self-limiting beliefs prevent you from enjoying your life's journey.

Don't worry about what others are going to think of you if you don't meet their expectations of you, on or off the mat. The truth is, one day you are going to die! Do you think when you die people are going to say, *"He lost that tournament... He failed on his business venture... What a disappointment!"* No! Because it does not matter!

Remember, the most common regret of, *"The Top Five Regrets of the Dying"* book:

> *"I wish I'd had the courage to live a life true to myself, not the life others expected of me."*

Don't let your dark passenger control your life, You must learn how to keep that voice in check. When you learn how to control your mind instead of letting your mind control you, you can accomplish amazing, meaningful things.

ENJOY THE JOURNEY, because life is short and it goes by fast. Enjoy it to its fullest!

These are pictures with my son Jonathan Dantas at the 2010 International Masters Championship in Rio De Janeiro, Brazil and in 2015 Speaking at the AZ Bodybuilding State Championship in Phoenix. It was the first time he saw me competing and the first time he saw me speaking live. If you want to share this philosophy of consistently challenging yourself, going out of your comfort zone, and becoming the best version of yourself, you must walk the walk.

– Gustavo Dantas

ABOUT THE AUTHOR

Photo: John Cooper

GUSTAVO DANTAS

is a fourth degree Black Belt in Brazilian Jiu-Jitsu from Andre Pederneiras. With nearly 20 years of coaching experience and being a World Class competitor, Gustavo is a public speaker as well as a Certified Mental & Life Coach with a bachelor's degree in physical education from UFRJ (Universidade Federal do Rio de Janeiro). Gustavo left Brazil in 1999 with a couple thousand dollars, two bags and one teenage dream: to have his own 100% Jiu-Jitsu Academy and to make his living through the passion of his life, Jiu-Jitsu. The Gustavo Dantas Jiu-Jitsu Academy was established in Tempe, Arizona on March 6, 2012, reinforcing the statement, *"Believe in yourself, believe in your dreams. Hard work pays off."*

Gustavo was the Jiu-Jitsu coach of the Mixed Martial Arts Gym, Arizona Combat Sports for 11 years, where he achieved his 2-0 MMA Record. During that time, Gustavo started the mission of promoting Jiu-Jitsu in the state of Arizona, becoming the Vice-President of the Arizona State Brazilian Jiu-Jitsu Federation and turning a small, 40-competitor, in-house tournament in 2001 to an impressive 700 competitors in 2011, which has helped Arizona to be recognized as one of the Jiu-Jitsu power houses in the United States.

Well respected in the Jiu-Jitsu community, Gustavo is also the co-founder of the non-profit organization, *"Live Jiu-Jitsu"* that continues to build champions on and off the mat in Arizona. Gustavo hopes to spread his coaching philosophy to more Jiu-Jitsu practitioners around the world for years to come through his program, *"Inner Discovery for Outer Success."*

> *"I want to help people perform to the best of their abilities and reach their full potential on and off the mat. I struggled with performance anxiety before, and I was able to overcome it using the techniques that I share in my program. These concepts, fundamentals, and techniques helped me, and I believe this program can help others too."*
>
> – Gustavo Dantas

Gustavo turning his "How high can you fly?" project into reality at the 2015 Adult World Championship in Long Beach, California.
Photo: Mike Calimbas

Gustavo expanded his horizons as a guest speaker at the 2015 AZ Bodybuilding Championship.
Photo: Nick Colvill

COMPETITION ACCOMPLISHMENTS:

- 2x ADCC Veteran (2001 & 2003)
- 2015 IBJJF Zurich International Open Silver medalist (Black/Adult/Light) Zurich, Switzerland
- 2015 IBJJF Gothenburg International Open Bronze medalist (Black/Adult/Light), Gothenburg, Sweden
- 2015 IBJJF Rome International Open Bronze medalist (Black/Adult/Light), Rome, Italy
- 2015 IBJJF Munich Winter International Open Silver medalist (Black/Adult/Feather), Munich, Germany
- 2014 IBJJF World Masters Silver medalist (Black/Master 2/Feather), Long beach, California
- 2014 IBJJF Long Beach International Open Champion (Black/Adult/Feather), Long Beach, California

- 2014 IBJJF U.S. National Champion (Black/Master 2/Light), Torrance, California
- 2014 IBJJF Vegas Spring International Open Champion (Black/Master 2/Light), Las Vegas, Nevada
- 2014 UAEJJF Abu Dhabi World Pro Jiu-Jitsu Champion (Black/Master 2/feather), Abu Dhabi, U.A.E.
- 2012 IBJJF World Champion (Black/Master 2/Feather), Long Beach, California
- 2012 IBJJF U.S. National Champion (Black/Master 2/Feather), Torrance, California
- 2010 IBJJF Vegas International Open Champion (Black/Master 1/Feather), Las Vegas, Nevada
- 2010 IBJJF International Master & Senior Champion (Black/Master 2/Feather), Rio de Janeiro, Brazil
- 2009 JJFJ Rickson Gracie International Champion (Black/Adult/Light), Tokyo, Japan
- 2008 CBJJ Brazilian National Champion (Black/Light/Master 1), Rio de Janeiro, Brazil
- 2002 CBJJO World Cup bronze medalist (Black/Ultra Heavy/Adult), Rio de Janeiro, Brazil
- 98 & 99 Joe Moreira International Champion (Brown & Black/Adult), Costa Mesa, California
- 98 FJJRJ Rio de Janeiro State champion (Brown/Feather/Adult), Rio de Janeiro, Brazil

- 97 & 98 IBJJF World champion (Purple & Brown/ Feather/ Adult), Rio de Janeiro, Brazil
- 97 CBJJ Campeonato Brasileiro por Equipes Champion (Purple/ Light/ Adult), Rio de Janeiro, Brazil
- 96 IBJJF World Championships Bronze medalist (Purple/ Light/ Adult), Rio de Janeiro, Brazil

If you would like more information about Gustavo's four-disc DVD, *"Inner Discovery for Outer Success"* available on demand, please visit www.thebjjmentalcoach.com